The Unhurried School Year

The School Year Survival Guide
for Moms and Dads

KAT SANFORD-CREARY

The Unhurried School Year
Copyright 2020 – Kat Sanford-Creary

Printed in the United States of America

Editing by: Jill Muñoz
Cover Design: Nabin Karna
All photographs by Ken Rada

The Unhurried Woman
Lawrenceville, GA 30044
theunhurriedwoman@outlook.com

Visit the author online at
www.theunhurriedwoman.com

Dedication

To my maternal grandparents, Leo and Evern Sanford
My paternal grandmother, Alice Taylor
and my aunt, Lorinda Kay Sanford.

The lives that you lived are still creating ripples.
I am grateful for every moment that I had with you
and I know that you are watching over me.
You are missed every single day.
I love you.

-k.

Foreword

Let's be honest; mom life is the best life. Here are these little people in your life who love you unconditionally. But, if you blink your eye twice ... their tweens and teens and that unconditional love comes with new standards! And, you stand there and say: "Where did the time go?" This is where I am in my life a mom of teens.

You don't have to wonder where the time has gone anymore because my sister has written this book to help moms, dads and parents everywhere stop rushing through parent life and become intentional in organizing your family life! You no longer have to feel like it just flew by! Take in every moment. Cherish those just-because hugs and hand drawn pictures. Take a few deep breaths and record the moments with your family with your eyes and not your phone!

Preplanned parenting is not the step you follow before having children, it's the precious few moments a week you spend time organizing your family life, so you can be present in every precious moment!

Stop rushing and live unhurried!

Deborah A. Montgomery

"An unhurried sense of time is in itself a form of wealth."

-Bonnie Friedman

Contents

Preface

Have you ever heard the saying that adding a third child is like you're drowning and someone says "Here. Hold this baby?" In our case, it was completely true. Our first two children were long-past potty training and waking up during the night. They had moved on to reading independently when we found ourselves pregnant with our third child. Currently, our children are 13, 10 and 5. Our oldest son is in 7th grade, our daughter is in 5th, and our youngest son is in Kindergarten. In addition to school, we are navigating through afterschool activities, sports, and scouting schedules. My husband and I both work fulltime jobs outside of the home and regularly serve in our community and church. I operate two home-based businesses of my own. We are a busy family. So, I know exactly how you feel when it comes to managing daily life and parenting well—it feels like there aren't enough hours in the day.

For the past nine years, I have been blessed to work in a Christian elementary and middle school as the office manager. I have had the opportunity to see and assist families navigating "all of the things" up close. Because I am like the parents that I serve, I am "in the trenches" and trying to overcome the exact same struggles that come with balancing several schedules at once. For the most part, I think I did a pretty good job of keeping track of everything at home and at work. I kept a basic calendar and kept it up to date; I also hung a wall calendar in our kitchen for the rest of my family to reference. About three years ago, I started to think that I needed something more substantial, especially since my oldest children were participating in more activities, and my youngest was going to be in the same place as them in no time. I recalled that during the years that I worked in the hospitality industry, I managed my schedule using a Franklin Covey Planner, and loved how it kept me on track. I didn't want anything as formal as what I had used in the past, so I started asking around for recommendations. To my surprise, other women in our school community were also looking for planning systems to help balance their work and family lives. It was great to have a like-minded group to bounce ideas off of. In the end, I selected a planning system, began faithfully using it to manage our full family calendar, a busy year-round work schedule and both businesses. I also have systems in place to help me manage my projects, goals and even my health.

Improving the way that I navigated helped make our family life better, even during the more hectic seasons. I have been able to create systems that have truly helped us "win" the school year one day at a time. In this book, I share practical steps that you can take to win yours, too! There is not one thing in these pages that I do not practice. I am still learning and I am sure that as my children reach different stages, our systems will evolve, and as will yours. I hope that in these pages you will find at least one strategy that leads you to living an unhurried school year and ultimately, an unhurried life.

The beginning of the school year awakens all kinds of feelings: joy, excitement, anxiety, fear, and anticipation. This is true for both students and parents. Unfortunately, long lazy summers have become a thing of the past and the hectic pace of a school year has become the norm. Nowadays, it seems that as soon as we relax, it's time to begin again.   As parents juggling family life and work life is difficult enough. When other things like activities and school projects are thrown in, it is especially easy to feel overwhelmed. We manage, but are often counting down to school breaks just like our kids, if only to catch our breath, individually and as a family. But, it really IS possible to live an Unhurried School Year--one that is filled with deliberate action at a measured pace, not chaos. This book is filled with tools and resources to help you do just that. In these pages, you will find out how to map out the year ahead in a way that will give you peace of mind. With your plan in hand, you will be able to control the impact of things that seemingly pop up out of nowhere, because you will have a strategy.

This book has four sections. Each one has steps that will ultimately help you navigate this school year and those to come! The best part is that if you commit to the first three, the last one can happen with minimal effort. You will have to do some work on the front end, but you will find that it is totally and completely worth it in the long run! Here are the four steps:

1. Map out your calendar for the year
2. Create a dinner meal plan
3. Transfer responsibility
4. Create margin

Let's   **begin.**

Chapter 1:
Mapping Out Your School Year

Hear me: if you do not do any of the other steps, do THIS one! It is the lead domino and I start with it for that reason. Once you have a clear idea of what is happening when, you will gain more than you know. To complete this step, you must begin with a printed calendar. If you do not already have one, please email me to secure the digital resource pack for this book. You may use a digital calendar later, but it is best to have a clear visual first. This calendar will become your Master Calendar. Once you have it in hand, follow these steps:

1. **School Calendar**: Go through your child's school calendar month by month and add all school activities, events, and breaks to your Master Calendar. Be sure to note when report cards are scheduled to be issued. If your student has a class syllabus that includes major project deadlines or presentations, add those as well. If your student participates in extracurricular activities that have major events, note those dates, too.

2. **Family Calendar**: Add immediate family birthdays, anniversaries, and other annual celebrations. Are there any special events planned—weddings, graduations, vacations, reunions, etc.? If so, add those, too. Add any family milestone events that you are aware of.

3. **Work Calendar**: Are you aware of any major project deadlines at work? Do you have any specific business trips

planned? Will you be attending any conferences or conventions? Are there any times that you expect to be busier than normal at work? If so, note those windows of time. Does your business operate using a fiscal or calendar year? Are there any other significant events that you are aware of?

4. **Service Calendar:** Are you regularly committed to serve or volunteer in your church or community organization? Are there any events, conferences, or activities being sponsored by your organization that you will be involved in planning or volunteering for? If so, note those dates on your calendar.

5. **Recreational Calendar:** Do any members of your family participate on an athletic team or in an activity that has its own calendar? When does the season begin and end? Are there any scheduled auditions, games, competitions, tournaments, or events? If so, add them to your Master Calendar.

Use Your Master Calendar to Identify Your Hotspots

A hotspot is defined as "a place of significant activity or danger." For you and your family, a hotspot occurs wherever multiple events overlap. Hotspots are not hard to find. You probably saw the potential for conflicts as you created your Master Calendar. hotspots. In most instances, your hotspots cannot be eliminated. They can, however, be managed. And, it is much easier to manage them when you know that they are coming weeks and even months ahead of time.

Here's a quick example of how we manage a recurring hotspot for my family:

My son's birthday is right around report card time each year. We cannot change his birthday or the fact that it is the exact halfway point of our first semester. That means that there are often tests, papers and projects due during the week leading up to his birthday. To minimize stress on our family, we usually schedule celebrations for the weekend after his birthday, because it is more enjoyable to him and his friends because they are usually done with testing and quarter-end assignments. As parents, we also understand that we may need to be available to help our son if he needs us as he prepares for big tests and completes projects that may have been assigned. So, we try to avoid taking on major projects during the same time frame. It also helps us to identify when our children may need extra grace and encouragement because they are managing deadlines and teacher expectations that they may find stressful.

Knowing that there is a need to manage a hotspot does not in and of itself create a solution, but it does provide you with an opportunity to strategize.

Use Your Master Calendar to Create a Family Calendar

A family calendar is the cornerstone of your command center. It tells everyone what's going on, as well as when and who is involved. What you use is entirely up to you; that you use one is the game changer that you most need. There are two basic options:

1. **Family Wall Calendar**

   I am a big proponent of a wall calendar posted in an area that everyone in the family can see. This creates buy-in from everyone that is involved and impacted by what is happening within your household. It helps them to see where the family's hotspots are for themselves. It also gives you an opportunity to let your children participate in the family's strategy for busy seasons. When you say, "Looks like we have a busy week ahead of us. How can we help each other make it run smoothly?" When your children have the opportunity to take part in the overall plan, they will not only take pride in it, but will also execute that plan better.

2. **Family Digital Calendar**

   There are several options when it comes to family digital calendars. I have personally used Cozi and Google Calendar for my family in the past. They both have great features, as do several other calendar systems and apps. They all take time to set up. If you use Outlook, iCal or Google Calendar at work, I would recommend using the same (if possible) at home so that you do not have to duplicate your work. You have probably heard the saying: "Garbage in, garbage out." That applies to maintaining a digital calendar. If you do not load good information and keep it updated, it will not help you. If there are members of your family that do not or will not use a digital calendar system, I do not recommend this option.

Here is something that happened at my house one Saturday afternoon:

Me: Kids, grab your jackets and get in the car. We have to go!
Oldest kid: But where are we going?
Me: ☹
Oldest kid runs to our family wall calendar, looks at it, comes back.
Oldest kid: Are we going to a book signing thing?
Me: Yes! That's exactly where we're going. Thank you for checking!

It was a small victory, but still a win in my book.

Whether you use a paper or digital calendar is up to you. The bottom line is that you commit to the system overall and use it diligently. This one thing actually spills over into every other area of your life. When you flip through the pages of your Master Calendar, I bet that you can already predict when life is going to be more hectic, and now you actually have the opportunity to do something about it.

Chapter 2:
Creating A Weekly Dinner Menu For Your Family

I f you are currently or have ever followed a specific program for eating, then you know that meal planning is an absolute necessity if you have any intention of sticking to the plan. A meal plan will help you in two ways: it helps you grocery shop in an intentional way and answers the "What's for dinner?" question before it can even be asked. If you are not using a meal planner for your family, do NOT skip this section.

Myths About Meal Planning

Myth #1: They work best for people that don't work or that work from home.

Meal plans work best for everyone. You do not have to be home all day to put a healthy meal on the table. No one wants to stand in front of a stove all day, even if it's in the next room.

Myth #2: It is too complicated.

You do not have to spend hours looking up recipes and going through cookbooks. Build your meal plan with recipes that you know and that your family already enjoys. While it's nice to try something new from time to time, tried and true work best especially during the week. If you do not already load your freezer with prepped meals, and that process is not appealing, you do not have to start.

Myth #3: It won't work for us because we are always on the go.

These days, commuting families are busier than ever. And that is exactly why you need a plan! You do not have to plan every night of the week. You create a plan that works for your family. There will be nights that you end up with take-out, pizza delivery, and UberEats; plan for those nights. Also, no one is checking to see if you followed your plan for the week—so when you need to, change it. Being "on the go" is not a good reason to operate without a plan. It is a reason to create one.

Myth #4: I don't have time.

The ultimate purpose of a meal plan is to make better use of your time. Have you ever gone to the grocery store without a list and ended up with a full cart but nothing for your family to eat for dinner? Have you ever had a debate with yourself about whether you should stop by the store on the way home to pick up the items that you forgot or just pick up Chinese instead? Do you ever end up with multiple packages of the same item in your pantry? If you answered yes to any of these questions, then you absolutely have time to meal plan, because you are wasting time by not meal planning. In my experience I have less food waste, fewer unplanned grocery runs, and more time when I've planned well. If you do not have a slow cooker, get one! (And here's a tip: put it on overnight, not in the morning. If your mornings are anything like mine, they are not the best time to try and remember what needs to go into the crockpot. If you do it in the evening after dinner is done and the kitchen is being tidied up for the night, you have a bit more time. Then, you can turn it off when you wake up and go through the day knowing that dinner is done.)

Four Key Steps

1. **Select Recipes**

   Create a pool of recipes that are a combination of your family favorites, quick meals and recipes that you would like to try. If you're new to planning or coming into a busy time for your family, do not experiment with new recipes and ingredients.

2. **Plan your dinner menu for 1-2 weeks**

   If your family likes (or leaves) leftovers, give yourself a break and use that on your menu for at least one day. Also, think about your schedule. (We have one night each week that the kids literally have to eat in the car because one activity runs into the next. I don't plan anything for that day.) Does your family have a weekend tradition— like pizza on Friday, dinner at the mall on Saturday? Keep them alive and write them into your plan. Finally, if you need to shift things around, do it! Again, no one is coming to make sure that you follow the plan exactly.

A note for beginners and out-of-practice veterans: when you start out, I highly recommend that you plan two weeks at once. This will give you more meals to move around however you need to. It will also help you with grocery shopping.

3. **Make your list and hit the grocery store**

   Once you have your meals planned, write down what's needed for each entrée and note any sides. Once you've done that, check your refrigerator, freezer and pantry for each item that you need; make sure that there's enough for each recipe and check each item off as you go. What is more frustrating than starting to prepare a meal only to find that you don't have enough of a staple item? (Spoiler alert: Nothing.) After you've checked off what you have, make your shopping list and off you go. You have a comprehensive list to shop with and it will make that task much easier. This is where all of the power shoppers and coupon queens scour the ads for deals—if that's you, then go for it. Here's my thought: If I buy something that I don't use, it is a complete waste of money, so I will shop smart, but the bigger value is in shopping wisely. When you make a two-week plan, you will also see places to save on ingredients because sometimes there will be an overlap. For example: If I serve chili on Monday, I may have a baked potato bar a few days later—because both meals share toppings. And while there may not be enough chili to serve as a leftover entrée, there certainly may be enough to use as a topping on a potato.

4. **Execute your plan**

Now, follow your plan. Once you get the hang of it, add new recipes to your rotation. Search for slow cooker meals, sheet pan dinners and one-pot wonder recipes—there are Pinterest boards, websites and entire cookbooks devoted to both. When you hit a hotspot on your calendar, keep it simple because you already have enough going on. If you get off track, start over again. Whenever you need help or ideas, wander over to The Unhurried Woman on Pinterest for recipes and tips.

Chapter 3:
Transferring Responsibility

Say this out loud: "I cannot do it all and I will STOP trying!"

You have to let other members of your family help manage chores and projects around the house. Is everyone going to do things the way that you do it? Absolutely not. Do you need to let them do those things anyway? Yes. If you want everyone on the same page, then you also have to take time to train them. Look for checklists that your children can use when completing chores to ensure that they do the things that you need done. There is no limit to the number of websites that will give you a list of age-appropriate chores for each child in your home. Get your children involved in planning the dinner menu and have them help in the kitchen, too. This is a big step, and admittedly hard to do. Here are a few steps to help you:

1. Think about your household and make a list of things that only you can do.
2. Then make a list of things that you typically do, but others could potentially take care of.
3. Gather your tribe, set expectations, train and transfer items from the second list to members of your family.

A note about kids and chores:

When you are training your children to take over specific chores, remember this: it will take them 6-12 months to master the task. That is why you need a good checklist. During their training period, you will have to be patient and resist the urge to do it for them--which can be painful. But, it will be worth it. They gain life skills and you get help around the house. Here is a great accountability method to use with siblings:

Your children have been trained to clean the bathroom, using your family's specific checklist. When it's Child One's turn to clean the bathroom, they do so using the checklist. Once they are done, Child Two inspects their work. Once that inspection is done, a parent inspects the work. Here's the best part: if the parent finds anything on the checklist undone, Child Two has to correct it.

Transferring responsibility is probably the hardest one for most moms, but the reality is that it's arguably the most necessary. I have said to my family many times: I need YOU to help with the things that anybody can do so that I can do the things that only I can do. You may need to adopt that statement, too.

Chapter 4:
Create Margin

argin is defined as: the rest that is built into your everyday life. The space between your load and your limit. Margin is the opposite of overload. With the demands of our daily lives, we often find ourselves running at maximum capacity while craving margin in one way or another. The less margin we have, the more stressed and frustrated we become. We are headed toward burnout when what we really need is room to breathe. We need margin, but it is not given, it is created by the choices that we make each day. Choose to plan your days well, and you will probably find that you have pockets of time that you previously may have misused. Choose to plan your meals well and you will save money, eat healthier, and spend time around the dinner table with your family. In what areas would you like to have more margin in your life? What adjustments can you make each day that will impact those areas?

Schedule Intentional Downtime

You have probably heard the phrase, "You can't pour from an empty cup. Take care of yourself first." It sounds great, and it even has a ring of truth to it. But we keep trying to do it, don't we?

Downtime absolutely, positively has to be scheduled just like everything else that you want and need to do! When you look at your calendar and see an open date, do not put anything there. Put YOURSELF on your schedule and commit to keeping the appointment. When there are events or activities that you want to attend, put them on your calendar early and work around them instead of trying to squeeze them in later. When you have an open day on your calendar, resolve to keep it that way! I recommend that you put "Do Nothing" days on your family's schedule at least once per month. It is perfectly okay, and sometimes, it is exactly what you need.

Self-Care

Self-care has become a popular term over the past few years. Eventually, it will stop being on magazine covers, blog posts, and talk shows, but that will not change the fact that it is very necessary. Self-care does not have to be a trip to a day spa; it could be a couple of uninterrupted hours walking around Target or treating yourself to a cup of coffee and a good book. Self-care is the practice of taking an active role in protecting one's own well-being and happiness. It is a practice that needs to be a part of your routine.

H opefully, you will take the practical steps outlined in the first three chapters of this book and use them to create routines for your family. They all work together to help you create margin with respect to time and money. Once you have created some breathing room by being more deliberate with your time I sincerely believe that other things will fall into place and this school year and the ones to come will truly feel unhurried.

Acknowledgements

First, I would like to thank my Lord and Savior, Jesus Christ, without whom I could do absolutely nothing.

This book would never have been possible without the help and guidance of the following people. I am overwhelmed with gratitude for their love, support, influence and contribution to my life. There is no doubt that you have all been placed in my life by God to encourage, challenge, correct, and build me into the woman that He created me to be.

To my children Kaleb, Rebekah and Seth--you have taught me more about life and love than I would have ever expected. You are the why that I never knew that I needed. It is an honor and a privilege to be your mom.

To my mom, Shelaine Sanford, thank you for all of the love, time, attention, laughs and support throughout my life. Mother-daughter game nights, movie marathons, shopping, soapy shoes, and that one surprise party pepper my memories, and still brings me to tears with laughter. Your resilient spirit and strong character have taught me so much about the kind of person I want to be. I love you.

To my dad, Kenneth Taylor, from playing backgammon, watching Fred & Ginger or Fernwood Tonight, laughing at bad jokes, and doing the "Curly Shuffle" all over Detroit, to deep conversations about books and scripture, you have been there. I can only hope that you know how much I love and appreciate you.

To my bonus-mom, Renaulta Taylor, you have always been an awesome support and I am so grateful that God blessed me with you. He knew that you were exactly what I needed. I cherish the times that we have shared during your solo visits to Atlanta. Thank you for always saying yes.

To my other parents, Huntley & Serenita Creary, I have learned so much from both of you! Your strength, determination and commitment to family and friends is a blessing to everyone that knows you. You both have amazing stories and should be writing books of your own!

To my sister, Deborah Montgomery, thank you for your encouragement and support. You are the best sister ever! You are a dynamic powerhouse and I cannot wait to see what the next chapter in your story holds for you. I love you.

To the women in Atlanta that surround me —you are an amazing village and I could never do all that I do without your help! Christina Alston, Brenda Conley, Amanda Dance, Catharine Jordan and Courtney Stanley, I thank you.

To the Detroit Public School teachers of Keidan Elementary, Bates Academy and Renaissance High School. It was a privilege to learn from the very best. What I gained from each of you goes far beyond classroom lessons. Thank you for all that you instilled in me.

To the faculty, staff and families of Victory World Christian School—I truly love you and I am grateful to be counted among you. I especially want to thank Irene Prue for selecting me to be a part of such an amazing community.

To Jill Munoz, you are a gift and a blessing. Thank you for always being available to edit my blog posts and book pages. (I didn't give you this section, so if it's a mess, it's on me.) I am grateful to have you as a friend and confidante.

To Yvette Mackey & family, the way that you have had our family's back is nothing short of extraordinary. The blessing that you have individually and collectively been to us all is overwhelming to even think about and hard to put into words. Thank you for all of the ways that you have and continue to contribute to our lives.

To Christine Harris, Mildred Patrick, Debra Davis, Annette Mooreman, Evelyn Moore, Ramona Sipes, Ann Lindsay, Carol Griffin, Crystal Banks, Tava Musial, Kasaundra Rogers, MaryAlice Bush, and Kara Nelson. I do not know how to properly express my love and gratitude to you all for teaching me so much about what it means to be a Godly woman. Each of you placed something different into my heart and those pieces help to make me who I am today. I am forever grateful.

I am blessed to be a partner in the great community known collectively as Reveal Church. I am grateful to Pastors Rolando and Olivia Gonzalez and the entire Reveal family! It is a pleasure to serve among you.

To my partner in crime, Kelleen Basden. You have totally been a Godsend in my life. We collaborate on more things and in more ways than I would think possible. We laugh together, we cry together, we vent together and are even able to put each other in check when necessary. You challenge me to think bigger and I am better for it. I am grateful for you and Team Basden for all that you contribute to my life and to my family. Kreative Konspiracy for the win!

Carmen Stokes, who knew that sitting around talking in Mr. Tank's class during senior year in high school would build the foundation for a friendship and sisterhood such as this? Only God could have orchestrated such a beautiful combination—truly yin and yang, although I always forget which of us is which. The valleys and mountain tops of my life would have been much lower without you to pull me up and push me higher. Thank you for every encouraging word, every shared thought, and more importantly every power-packed prayer that you have sent up on my behalf.

Finally, to my husband, Reggie Creary, thank you for loving me fiercely and completely; for being the first to encourage and support me and for being the amazing force behind everything that I do. I am eternally grateful to God for uniting us as true partners in this thing called life. It is an honor to be your wife and there is no one that I would rather walk next to than you. Thank you for holding me up when I've been down, waiting when I'm not ready to talk and listening when I am. You are awesome, and I love you.

Those that know me know that one of my favorite verses in the Bible is Romans 8:28 which reads, "And we know that in all things God works for the good of those who love him, who have been called according to his purpose." There are many other people that have taught me something, spoken a kind word, or simply extended a hand a friendship to me. You have all made me who I am today: the author of this book. You have contributed to my life, to my good and to my purpose in Christ. Thank you.

Live Unhurried,

Kat

About the Author

Kat Sanford-Creary is a proud native of Detroit, Michigan. She currently resides in Atlanta, Georgia with her husband of over 20 years and her three children, ages 5 to 13. After a nearly fifteen-year career in the hospitality industry, she began working as an Office Manager in a private Christian school. She is a blogger, coach, workshop facilitator and will launch her podcast, The Unhurried Woman, soon. Kat is passionate about helping others create actionable plans and providing the accountability that they need to achieve their goals.

You can visit her at http://www.theunhurriedwoman.com or on Instagram, @theunhurriedwoman.

To receive information about her upcoming classes or events, please send an email to theunhurriedwoman@outlook.com.

Photo Credit: Ken Rada Photography